BARNEY ASHTON-BULLOCK

Café Kaput!

BROKEN SLEEP BOOKS

Published 2020,
Broken Sleep Books:
Cornwall / Wales

brokensleepbooks.com

First Edition

Lay out your unrest.

Publisher/Editor: Aaron Kent
Editor: Charlie Baylis

Typeset in UK by Aaron Kent

Broken Sleep Books is committed to
a sustainable future for our planet,
and therefore uses print on
demand publication.

brokensleepbooks@gmail.com

ISBN: 978-1-913642-06-8

Contents

Out of performance and theatrical music come rhythm, syncopation, balanced two-stress lines, drum-beat spondees, alliteration, almost Stabreim, sharp Anglo-Saxon - 'tart', 'swart' - ever startling constructions, inventive, not for a moment dull. The content is often rebarbative but always self-knowing: seductions, betrayals by chisellers and preening preyers on the innocent, the rejects, perennial victims of an unthinking self-pleasuring. O the 'flabster queens' and 'snuckers' and 'dotard whores' of a down-and-out bourgeois Britain, of Dorset hamlets left by the wayside, of superannuated B & Bs. O tempora o mores! 'Pathological narcissism' vies with 'the naïveté that's totally defeated me'. 'My signature shifts of register/and sonic tectonics of syllabic toss' confront the 'amnesiac emeritus goal of utterances unbound by metre or meaning'. This collection is hard, sad yet ecstatic; brilliant, awful, amazing and brave. *(Chip Martin, London, 2020)*

Barney and I, along with musician Chris Frost, make up the hybrid poetry, theatre and song collective 'Andy Bell is Torsten'. That project's undertow of mirthful, darkly poetic menace is brought into sharp focus in Barney's concise new poetry collection, 'Café Kaput!' Emotionally astringent observations, the poems in 'Café Kaput!' claw into the aching epicentre of the thwarted hopes, dreams and ambitions of our age. The 'against the odds' existence of weary souls on the margins of life, where fetish, fear and phobia coalesce. It celebrates the broken souls who cling to a desperate hope despite the overarching chaos and indifference of an often cruel, judgmental world. It is the stuff of nightmares, but not without a tender mercy; it really is the dog bollocks. Read it if you dare! *(Andy Bell of 'Erasure', London, 2020)*

Barney Ashton-Bullock's poetry in 'Cafe Kaput!' impacts like verbal weaponry. Viscerally raw, unflinchingly targeted, lyrically sensual, its tensions operate on the boundaries of an alliterative accent compounding street, palare and spiky self-invention with optimal dexterity. 'In sleek, sleety, diamanté's drawl' is how I read him, the soft and the hard burning bright on a mission. That mission is outsider poetry. Read this book. *(Jeremy Reed, London, 2020)*

Café Kaput!

Barney Ashton-Bullock

Done For

Probabilistic!
The minute that the mindset told me,
We, pop band, were *product*,
We were as quanta unbound
Wretching to wrung, strung, powdery scattering;
Done in with the knowledge,
And done for.

Joggers

The strewn, stricken, jilted joggers
befilthed, enlittering encrusted carpets
and I smunch / trawl through the gaits and girths of all
in scuba search of the pearls conched within
of turdy streaked keks and jammy socks
to boil wash
such is my glee to be
a licky, licky retriever
getting a modicum of affirmation for such things
as lubricant to scant pleasantries
instead of unfathomable, distancing, mood swings
from Sir Lazyass about how I don't do a fukkin' thing

the swing an' bulge of his genital flopsies
seems to be his raison d'être
along with his untrue conceit
that no-one could love or fuck me better
and my raison d'être… oh, to help him forget her

First Time

The swarf hearts of swarthy queerio
Gigolo wannabe tarts
Swaying carefree down cruisey wharfs
They set upon the fresher meat
For self betterment
Butter up such fundament with lubing tongue
Wink at 'ring-a-ring-a-wanker' spurned voyeur suitors
Who, mid-thrum, give him the up-thumb
For filleting with such stentorian aplomb
The most beautiful virginal of us young'uns

And liked it...

The plaster board and base blue asbestos panels beneath
are sodden to a stout porridge and
listing with their murky sewage infested, polluted moistness and
thirsty me scrunches a fistful of the pulp and gulps at the
quenching drippage.
I know the taste, I bit asbestos tiles as a kid and liked it…

Alone

Evanescent timeslip
The thwarting curfew
The ravishing hunger from feast day fastings
The latitudes of deities
Their promise of presence ever deferred.

Your juddering, skittish heart
Pickled in the desperation of chronic crush fatigue
Inconsequential replicated frivolities
Of exhaustingly toxic hook-up lines
Your contorted bitch-face at rest only in sleep.

There's the shame in your sleeping alone
The respite of bitterness
The pit-stop pause of snooze
The only counter to the truth of you
That, serially rejected,
The kick-in, hackling ego attacks to defend
And you always, always lose
Before anyone could even choose
You to, perhaps, be their lover, husband, friend.

Men

Men as lovers were never friends,
They were warmth and noise
And provision and demand;
Their 'suit behaviour' as if an erasure
Of the private world they lived in
Fleetingly with me
While separated, by degrees,
From their truer nature.

The Bros of UnMersey

Mssrs doing smash-grab, slow-grip, throat-choker thing;
A slappety mouth, yappety, yobbety, mugging, mauling!
Spent puffball, buffed-up flabster queens hithered,
Soon skittling as guttered scum a-flailing;
Stomped bauble beauties 'midst mirthy me-ow drawlings!

Cross fade to coke-stoked guffaws of tomcats' serrating screechios,
Cracked falsetto jubilations, clawing out mugged Muggins purse
Their wallets liberated to prolong team libation.

"20 quid more for a glam-slam gram fellas!"
Face slasher scowls abound afore:
Hearsehole fundament bootings as a jacksy's lubing
Prior to t'taunting, *"wanna taste fistings?"*
Enfrazzed in frenzied whippety
Pre and selfie-posing post-coital cursings…

"Fukkin' reaped it!"
A shared cigarette,
A mulched mayo chip 'n' dip pack-munched...

Blood soaked splotching on four quid throwaway Primark shirts
Worn from the cellophane without ironing
Used as offal bibs in sequential alley fuck'n'chuck fightings:
Chocked and clocked, the slain's feint fearsome weeping,
And to think such thuguli e'er made love to anything
Or that any young man bought them drinks hoping…

Unbidden

Commercial temperance hotel
Tots of teetotal Sasparilla
And soft supped shots of hot coffee
Pipe smoke masks a third latent fart threading its wrank way
through the feathered cushions
Betwixt settee slumberers dossing in the umbra thrown
around a candle lit reading room

Rigorous excision of whispered drifts of idle cant
By a maiden aunt steeped in the Manchester Guardian
Such upstandees uphold the bold wall painted command of
'Silence!'
In undulating eye darts of 'Shush!'
While the fob watches in murmurous choral tick
Lick at the static air, unbidden

Sezincote

I've measured my days in summer fêtes that fade,
Annual tombolas, a Stromboli of remembrance;
The cheese, the wine, the bracelets we won,
As in another life, my Cotswolds one.

Apple-bobbing, mirth filled miscreants,
A tour of the grand house; *"No heels on the parquet!*
No fingers on the paintings!
And stay, if you will, on the carpet protectors!
And the banquettes are antiques and not for lounging,
Though the velveteen sheen does seem inviting!"

"The historic collection of monogrammed decanters are over there
to view
With the family crested canteens of cutlery,
And much elbow grease needed to clean that lot, fuck you!"

The Orangery where we ate homemade cake and drank wan tea,
Where the maitre'd overheard my hashed plea
That I thought it best you marry me.

You, flustered that our fête-won, wax encased prize cheese,
Of which there were three in a Fine Fare presentation box,
Might soon get hot, were we not
To wend our way back to the train;
It was, thus, you'd skirt mention of my heart's intention
And I knew we'd not see Sezincote again.

In Cruisers' Creek

In Cruisers' Creek, my salt lake Jesu
Seeps set-piece, septic, pre-cum coronas
In sleek, skeety, diamanté drawl
All auroric oxidised with prawny aroma
Through nylon shorts and ill-laundered screes of scrimmy sheets
In sauna booths where spent sheaths crackle underfoot
Like arid autumn leaves
To testify the fertility/virility of virtual strangers
And all the lies mutually croaked by spunktious lined throats
As sequential ear-worm *amuse-bouches entrées* of pricktease
Devant les bricolage des periodic tables of potential STDs

Volte-Face (About Face)

Psoriasis of the sphincter
put an end to the chirrup of wild abandon
lest one eczmatic lava crack erupt
the folds of bloodied cack attack again
and the stench corrupt the fragrant windwhistles
into stormy eclectic invective

I'll stay unslain
snugly bound in my 2-for-1 chainstore knickers
slathered discreetly beneath
with Canestan and Daktacort
to ameliorate whatever
my fair slut bucket's re-caught
by means of the naïveté that's totally defined me
as so invert introvert, so inert

A supplicant initiate
to the wanton users of a world perverse
their daisy-chain, dick chase of flophouse flip-arse without a
face
sidelined anew, crimped of night urges, I slur homeward
I slobber to shivering mother how, *"I will not be a mistake"*
she sips her cup-a-soup and stokes the trash in the grate

She burrs I be;
"stricken in a porno stew of old roux
that you do
too greatly stir, young sir"

Unpinned niche erotica adrift in vortices of pixel rifts
That radiate their briney starburst pfaffs 'cross dying screens
Such modem brokered bit torrent dreams veneer this un-
kempt mind
It's fitful digital flak scouring its rapidity of protraction
Misshapes form in the static and dissolve,

Shapeshifters, emergent, decay before they bless
To lead I, their tethered charge, to a broken righteousness
Through corridors of the lie, *"Volte-face"* (about face)

Odd Oeufs (de Saint-Denis)

Ecstatic exits...... *Vendredi!*
Misaligned tropes....... *Samedi!*
Who'll void the gyre come *Dimanche?*

Metronil peddlers hawking shadows,
The rejected penitent mastic perspire;

Viva l'assemblage of husked soul eggshells
Smulched to fag ashen grain
A jackbooted silty *compresse* in the pavement cracks
of *les grandes boulevards,*
A slur of arid sediment waiting for rain…

Or *Pastis,* or piss,
Beside *la Seine.*

Anteroom

In anteroom fester, the draught swung pendant lamp
flickers the nibbed shadows of mildew fronds
to distend down warped, damp, woodchipped walls.

Powdering tomes of inspirational verse
mâché in our ferreting fingers.
We await the clicking tannoy's sputtered instruction;

"Your weaknesses, your sins and your issues
did not make the shortlist.
Disperse! Disperse!
O, derivative verse!"

Emeritus

amnesiac emeritus
you'd versify profanity
you'd hull the husks of student souls
supplicant pupils in the serried ranks of schoolroom desks
erased without trace
not sold on your goal
of utterances unbound by
metre or meaning

diphthongs serially elongated beyond the breath
for irritant effect
any assonance in the dissonance
cleft to the phrenic shred of pseudo-words
thought misheard by ass-licker sidekicks
who never deigned to say 'excuse me'?
or 'pardon me'?

a Phyrric victory of misshapen sorts
this cadence of nonsense slaw
this pasting of gibberish into the brains
of sycophants on the make
who can't contain their fake feelings
that I can still amaze and yet be so
out of time and out of place

my signature shifts of register
and sonic tectonics of syllabic toss
enunciated nonsense pronunciations
in meaningless skiffle sift like my life
now might we enjoy silence
and amnesia and dementia
as an eminent emeritus should

Motel Strange

Wotcha m'putrid popsicle!
Sorry the sherbet pips got wet.
Was those lolloping licks at the 'Welcome Desk'
Like the motel staff's tongues all had palsy
Slurping a rippling slurry of saliva into my knapsack

Also, I'd bathed in the semenous sugarplumulus clouds
Of a daft brush suitor on an overnight
He attempted seduction, bless it
Hefting about for an angle, as he'd not done ass before
Used to missionary I guess…
I wanked once he'd left.

Radipole - Out Of It (Deluxe)

Omnishambolic… The gruelly spermbursts from our kicked
bollocks;
The native Dorset daughters shy away.

Aortal anthems of ad hoc four letter words slurred into a timeless
rectitude;
Pisshead, jackboot, thugggery, yes!
Yet, as a pastiche potage of a 'crew',
Assumed, assuredly, a bit o'ruff deluxe;
This loose, shapeshifty, bitumen brew,
This assemblage of chummy loners and losers, true!

We speak in oddments and oddities of the Anthropocene age.
Casements of spent vials of home brew, knock-off shots,
Mad Dog 20/20 translucent with our flotsam slobber;
Our platitudes of jabs and right hooks,
Applied with affection betwixt we skittling punchdrunk
Who laugh at contusions and the serenity of knockout.

Now the curfew is ladling down like a vomitous broth
And our matedoms clutch in the crannies of the distil points of
derelict quarters
With whatever dregs aswill in our filtched tinnies
Supped as we smutch for scant warmth
And chirrup in fractal glitch; out of it.

Thirty year train wreck later, this be redolence deluxe
As I flob into Radipole lake.

Guttered delinquents, mastic seep; inelegantly, inexpertly spatch-
cocked.
Tenderised in the bootstomp, scabs crisping in the coiling night;
Darkly mottling bruisings, black as the potholed tarmac sur-
rounds.

Eternal trimesters of trial.
Our forged crunk credentials; misfiring misspells in faltering scrawl.

You slagged us for loitering in Arndale arcades,
Those arcades now padlocked empty!
We could've been crests of swans glissing 'cross the Radipole lake,
But got slated and slaked into the quicklime slime
Of your aloofly, boggle-oggle, judgmental stares:
Quagmired Dorset lads for whom quarries, trawlers, farmsteads
And grockle laden summer seasons were no longer there.
Not we, beshillinged, cart-bound chancers a-chance to reel merrily down Ridgeway
Nor the clobber and pat to seduce a Lizbie Brown,
Just shat, pissed keks and hunkery hovels in what of Budmouth Regis be left.

We sleep beneath fresnels of rot fronds in watery basements:
On sponge damp mattresses, we, attired in gaffa'ed cast off carrier bags to stay dry,
Marinaded in the stupor stews of drunken weedheadedness,
Out of it.

Guest House

Busy with dizzy splay of trite word play,
Porch full of fading, feigned maxims,
"Arrive as strangers, part as friends…..",
All thoughts of such dreary word-wank consort
Could have the mildest mannered guest,
Whether the 'good lady wife' or her hen-pecked man,
Resort to the brusquest brush off, "fuck off!"
And, preferably, if so aggrieved, just as fast as they flippin' can;
For I still limply proudmouth all out t'door,
"Come again won'cha, auf weidersehen!"
Because, "See you soon is not goodbye!"
And a guest house landlady must stockpile her little white lies
For visitors to Bridlington are now all the harder to come by
Since the regular holiday trade died
With the closure of steelworks, fisheries and mines,
We, bay-window shuttling, chamois shine the mottled Deco glass
For those who shuffle by
To shufty in it to straighten hair, coat, hat, tits, tie.

It all went wrong when booking.com
Cornered the reservations for most UK accommodation
And Trip Advisor replaced the word o'mouth of m'regular, B&B
seasiders
Who'd perhaps not travelled as wide or as far
To imbue their reviews with the nous of the worldly-wise
Who fabricate faults as if connoisseurs who'd freely despise
All but the very best of the best.
Their rarified tastes, opinions and choices, once online,
They assume will reflect
Oh, so well upon their penny-pinching lives!

Tarot Cards As Thrown

the tarot cards as thrown
upset, are torn, disowned
for we are gasping in the filthy flotsam
in an anarchy of arcana
in our outpost, post-Arcadian lives
skittering amidst the disjoints
of the remnants of an Albion
that fell

and those astute and adept
do tell of the perversity
that in adversity
is when this Isle does so well

those of us hectored, hassled few left
toil in the verdant vistas and views despoiled
by despots who desecrated with bombshell craters
and mass graves
who shepherded the exodus
who marmalised dissent
into an opposition as pliable as a warm, wan margarine
and as servile as the cart grease
dolloped on the wheels of their flagrant and fascist ambition

internal exiles, we collude in their curfew
and, by daylight, scratch at the soil
soothsaying for sustenance to come
to feed our young
for we're all undone,
scorched all as we were
by the now burnt up blinding brilliance
of a momentary nuclear sun
it's immanent, impermanent radiance raining down
it's poison and pestilence and disease
and us fucked foot soldiers left

forlornly beg, "please!"
for the card of death to be dealt by
the tarot cards as thrown

I Cannot Deal With Praise Today

Scraunched in an apoplexy of freeze,
A twinkling ice monstrance lands askew and the thud cracks
the eucharist porthole
Ejecting the customary archaic sop of the 'Body Of Christ'.
It appears as a compact anaemic flying Askey's wafer.
It spontaneously combusts in swirly fork-tongued gusts
And fragments in the emergent smash-mouth cyclone.
We dob out our own spoon tongues in desperate expectancy
For as long as we can avoid them freeze-drying in the wonk
of the 'wind chill factor'.
We're all ecumenically, if dementedly, attempting to entice to
our valuable lickety spittle,
A scrump of his transfiguring dust that might just deliver the
miracle of thaw,
That the sun might nudge in stabby shard to slay the deathly
overcast 'Hooded Claw'.
Who knew that the enfrazzlement would call so very many
But choose so very few?

Shoscombe

There is one of the iron reinforced concrete pilings left underneath the thick vegetation on the embankment and you can see it sometimes during a very severe winter if it's been stormy enough to whip away the weeds and leaves and twigs but, other than that, there is nothing left of any of the supports and stanchions that held up the prefab slabs of the long demolished, longer closed platforms of our local wayside halt. Of course, you may wait for a train but, I'm afraid, the alignment would need to be re-surveyed, the railway line would have to be rebuilt, the station summarily reopened but, the track bed, I'm afraid, has been severed in many places and all the staff are dead and they don't have steam trains anymore so, you might have a bit of a wait. While you wait, may I suggest that we fall in love and that you might not want to leave Shoscombe again? There's a Viennese Finger left in the pantry, and I can always send Roger out to get some more.

i pray from god my soul escapes

an expansive, cinematic bravado;
bawdy, iambic, barrack mess banter.
the assertive chivalry of opening bottles on molars:
human vassal states in klonky sidewalk *'klompendanse'*.

"lovely stag attire, cunt:
could do with a splash more colour!"
and sabre cuts a skein of ruby red
around a radial arc of neck.

Snuck

the addict supplicant wafers into the den,
her wan coded morse rap on the shuttered mesh
and the dealer yells, "Penetrate!"

injectable cruelty without beauty awaits;
penumbral dig of ammonium waft skag
to adroitly slag about fluvial sand-drag veins.

the leaden cleft of spaced out heft
and she's pawed again in a titty bar,
spooled around on a swivel stool;

spooged orifi apportioned as
sweetmeat candy by the pound.
a snacky fuck's a 'snuck',
by deduction, dedication and by gestalt.

Frau Totton

Though aspirant of coiffure and couture
A wastrel wayfarer, you, to and through
All the dismal darknesses of the world
Will there be one murk to befit or fit
This mental slipshod
This sentient landslip
I am immuring beneath, now that I'm 'getting on a bit'
To chunter-chat such schmaltz and chintz and shit
About much missed times I never lived

Prise the blighted, bloomed bolts from betwixt the kiosk's sever-
ally rusted shutters
The flaps scarred with decayed staple lattices
Remnants of once hastily affixed handbills
Offering this or that service or product or body
Some fabulously handwritten, neat as a Letraset appliqué
Offering pot-pourris of ways to get laid, straight and gay
Though mostly are scrawled and misspelt in biro brio
And hastily posted to desperately sell
The ass-end or cunt of a narcotised, narky, ne'er do well
Frittata faced emaciates, greasy sebum their pomade
All scabs and scabies amidst the plenitude of genital warts
Their professional hazard, our humbling cunt-punter after-
thought;
Passé porn princess 'pustulising',
The bingo wing sweat so surprising
Running in its welty rivulets

Totton's tottering totties teetering legs spread across the missing
floorboards
Now we've found a bleak bolt-hole HQ to 'do' you,
To bomb-rush bum this sorry slop of dotard whores
Their success will be addressed solely in terms of their ease of ac-
cess
And we'll use their sticky, stinky, fuzzy, faux furs
As our makeshift make-out mattress

From nubile to nuked
From fucking fit and fit to fuck
To comatose in puke

The once plenty shilling
Earned by trilling filth and tit-fuck thrilling
Was it salted away
For these years of Sundays that
You loiter by the tumbler's warmth in the laundromat
And make your free Waitrose cuppa'tea last from twelve to three
And dawdle by hand dryer heat in dusk-lit cemetery lavatories

For those none too choosey 'bout the holes they'll stick
You still ad hoc perform your tonguey, todger-tickling tricks
And pour maple syrup in the concavities of your lolloping tits
As your vendees excuse to lick
Every inch and crevice of your drop-stitch cellulite
For further fivers you'll piss away long before dawn light

•

Pathological Narcissism

Oh, that blithe darkling
Can e'en soothsay, via his verbose stitch-up bitchings!

In his murmurating foment of doggerel, a multiplicity of
conflictions witnessed
Amidst the blissful eddies he projects of an eternal/universal
matedom.

He refracts an auroric divine
In the blasé bosh-bosh of his deft panhandling oratory;

A consummate knife-twister, adrool in a seeming sexual
salivation,
He chocks the poisoning piling deep in your back,

Mere foundation into which he'll pour a caustic concrete
viciousness
To set to a septic, helpless stasis and maul hope to a static turgidity,

Yet, laughing rootlessly all the while,
And so manically aflutter, the batting of his avuncular eyes!

I long bade farewell to that humming narcissus
Rotweilling his bingo hall bonhomie, his Z-list showbiz canker,

His ad hoc distemper drolled with a gargoyle's aplomb
In verbal gush of crass guff, a wound of words adroitly served
As if aerodynamic motile swerves;
As if gliding curtain hooks on daring hairpin curves
On a glitter slash curtain rail in a life drawing class
Sparkly, smooth aswish apart on its rail
To reveal cellulite welt and bleeding bitten nails
And a motivational cue from the yawning 'teech'
To try to represent the life-cycle transition
From loaded 'it-girl' to stricken ne'er do well.

As the means to blueprint academic grade kudos
We empathically, but too suddenly, charcoal draw our slaw
Of those floodlit, still pulsing slain,

These once loved-up, love-bombed victims belatedly accursed
In a killing simper of his wretched words
Of his casually flung frequent fibs, to those he'd harass to fudge-
fuck knob-nib
With the scrawniest specimen, his tattooed pubis hearthed, flaccid
dick
Orgasming with the vibrative words *'Amigos para sempre.'*

So, excuse me if your evil I beget with an unwavering constancy!
Excuse me, if I don't applaud your vainglorious charade
And creep from such sham shags in a shush
Through alarmed fire exits to achieve, in time, a due clemency;
A rebound to a birthright of freedom; unbound from your vexa-
tious realms
To a stolid, reclusive, levity of mind.

I leave your crawing, clawing in yesteryear's bunged up behind
I will not be a milling maggot on anyone's pound of flesh!
In a rapture of exaltation,
In the sashaying subtleties
Of reawakened, sublime imagination,
He does not dwell in these faculties redivined,
For this is now *my* testimony, *my* mind, *my* time, is it not?

Who are you to cast aspersions to deign to redesign
Such epiphanic resolve?

And here you come straggling, lonely again,
Spurting your slur of third person apologia!

On whose authority do you shoehorn into my now deaf ears
Such unappealing appeasement
As some threadbare counterplot to freedom?

Acknowledgements

My thanks to the Soho Poetry Nights collective, to Richard Scott and Maurice Riordan of the Faber Academy, Chip Martin and John-Paul Pryor of the Mortimer House Speakeasy, Anne-Marie Fyffe and Cahal Dallat of Coffee House Poetry at the Troubadour, polymath poet and biographer Jeremy Reed and to Andy Bell and Chris Frost of our 'Andy Bell is Torsten' collective for seven fabulous years of pushing boundaries both on record and at the Above The Stag Theatre.

Thanks to the journals, blogs and anthologies that have published my works; the 'Avalanches In Poetry' collective celebrating Leonard Cohen, the Society Club Press for inclusions in 'Soho Nights' volumes 2 and 3 and for publishing my first collection 'Schema / Stasis : The Torsten Verse Diaries', New River Press, the Wellington Street Review (where 'Sezincote' was first published) SPAM zine (where 'Shoscombe' was first published) and the now defunct 'The Pandorian'.

Thanks to the poetry salons, festivals and open mic nights where many of these poems were first performed; the Wilderness Festival, Conrad Gamble's 'Ear Smoke' events, the Waddington-Custot Gallery, the Slipoff Festival, Betsey Trotwood (Curate's Egg), the Roughler Club, the Troubadour, the Mortimer House Speakeasy, Bedford Park Festival, Talking Rhythm, Jason Why's events at the Tea Tree Theatre, Celine Hispiche's celebratory 'Celine's Salon' readings and the Downes Braide Association for being their honorary poet.

To my inspirations Weldon Kees, Thomas Hardy, Harold Pinter, Sarah Kane, Steven Berkoff, Derek Jarman, Hannah Lowe, David Sylvian, the Redskins, Jonathan Meades, Kathryn Maris, Rupert Brooke and Marc Almond. And for Gianni Fontana without whom…

A final thanks to the fearless Broken Sleep Books crew for engaging with this work. To Aaron Kent & Charlie Baylis - *'keep on keepin' on!'*

LAY OUT YOUR UNREST

www.ingramcontent.com/pod-product-compliance
Lightning Source LLC
Chambersburg PA
CBHW071939020426
42331CB00010B/2944